SOFT COATED WHEATEN TERRIER

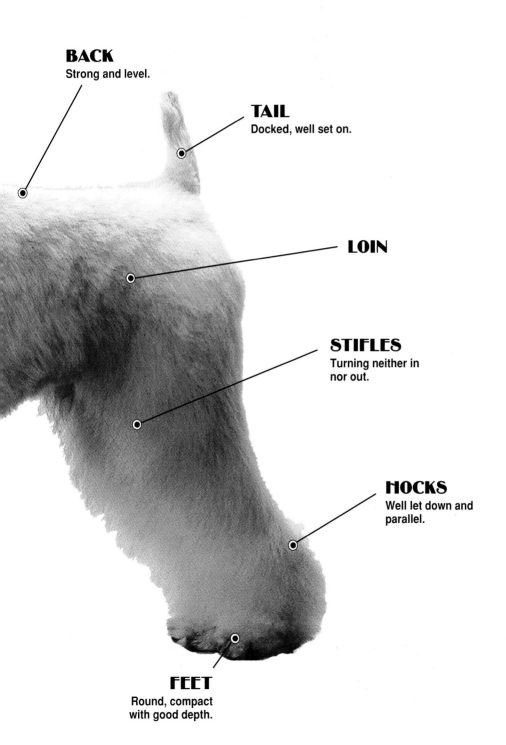

BACK
Strong and level.

TAIL
Docked, well set on.

LOIN

STIFLES
Turning neither in nor out.

HOCKS
Well let down and parallel.

FEET
Round, compact with good depth.

Title Page: Soft Coated Wheaten Terrier photographed by Robert Pearcy.

Photographers: Mary Bloom, Mary Ann Donahue, Gay Sherman Dunlap, Cheryl Turner Fogarty, Isabelle Francais, Jacqueline Gottlieb, Judy Iby, Robert Pearcy, Ron Reagan, Daniel and Marjorie Shoemaker, Elizabeth Sorenson, Judith Strom, Karen Taylor.

Distributed in the UNITED STATES to the Pet Trade by T.F.H. Publications, Inc., One T.F.H. Plaza, Neptune City, NJ 07753; distributed in the UNITED STATES to the Bookstore and Library Trade by National Book Network, Inc. 4720 Boston Way, Lanham MD 20706; in CANADA to the Pet Trade by H & L Pet Supplies Inc., 27 Kingston Crescent, Kitchener, Ontario N2B 2T6; Rolf C. Hagen Inc., 3225 Sartelon St. Laurent-Montreal Quebec H4R 1E8; in CANADA to the Book Trade by Vanwell Publishing Ltd., 1 Northrup Crescent, St. Catharines, Ontario L2M 6P5 ; in ENGLAND by T.F.H. Publications, PO Box 15, Waterlooville PO7 6BQ; in AUSTRALIA AND THE SOUTH PACIFIC by T.F.H. (Australia), Pty. Ltd., Box 149, Brookvale 2100 N.S.W., Australia; in NEW ZEALAND by Brooklands Aquarium Ltd. 5 McGiven Drive, New Plymouth, RD1 New Zealand; in Japan by T.F.H. Publications, Japan—Jiro Tsuda, 10-12-3 Ohjidai, Sakura, Chiba 285, Japan; in SOUTH AFRICA by Lopis (Pty) Ltd., P.O. Box 39127, Booysens, 2016, Johannesburg, South Africa. Published by T.F.H. Publications, Inc.

SOFT COATED WHEATEN TERRIER

A COMPLETE AND RELIABLE HANDBOOK

Marjorie C. Shoemaker

RX-140

CONTENTS

DESCRIPTION OF THE SOFT COATED WHEATEN TERRIER

From the land of mysterious druids, wailing banshees, and impish leprechauns comes a bundle of gold—the Soft Coated Wheaten Terrier.

The Wheaten Terrier of Ireland was bred to be a mid-size, multi-purpose farm dog and companion. In fact, a number of Wheatens would hunt badger to qualify for a Certificate of Gameness. In addition to being one of the first recorded Irish champions, Ch. Kingdom Leader, owned by Mr. Blake, acquired his Field Champion title, recognizing him as a "hunting dog."

The Soft Coated Wheaten Terrier was bred in Ireland as both a working dog and a companion.

Curiosity may have killed the cat — but it never stopped a Wheaten! Wheaten Terriers Missy, Liddy and Callie, owned by Marjorie and Daniel Shoemaker, demonstrate the breed's natural inquisitiveness.

The Irish farmers have always been practical. To this end, the Wheaten is an economy-size dog who is a sentry, cow-hand, farm-hand, occasional bird-dog, vermin destroyer, and family member who could exist on small portions of food. This requires intelligence, hardiness, endurance, versatility, and agility. Being Irish means being full of life and curiosity; being a Wheaten Terrier means having an irrepressible sense of humor, tireless enthusiasm, and a bounty of love for all people, especially his family.

Wheaten Terriers are devotees of the human race. Like Will Rogers, they feel a stranger is only a friend they haven't met. Their families are recipients of great leaps of joy and licks, welcoming them back, whether they are gone five weeks or five minutes. Their goal is to be a constant companion, a true member of the family. They will willingly accompany you in rain, hail, blizzards or boiling heat. They will pine for human companionship if left alone. They do not make good "kennel dogs."

Wheaten Terriers are noted for their intuitive understanding. There are many stories of Wheatens realizing physical frailties in people. This special ability makes them wonderful Therapy Dogs, for they become very docile and curb their natural tendencies to jump up and greet. This breed has long been used successfully in homes for handicapped children and nursing homes.

The Wheaten is a "quick study," with an uncanny ability to understand his human's moods and wishes almost before they do. Your Wheaten will have spent hours studying you while you thought he was napping. Wheatens are keen and willing participants of obedience, tracking and agility courses. The biggest problem owners must contend with is keeping their Wheatens from getting bored with the routine that was learned so quickly. I have put obedience titles on a few of my Wheatens and speak with some authority on this subject. A female we owned, named Amber, attained her obedience title but only after a few mistrials where she suddenly trotted off, once to say hello to the ring steward and another time to visit with the crowd. The male I worked with, Ian Harrigan,

The Soft Coated Wheaten Terrier's love for humanity is evident in the loyalty and affection he shows towards his family. Owners, the Donahue family.

putting him through his Companion Dog Excellent (CDX) title thoroughly enjoyed obedience work and had a very creative mind. He loved to vary the routine on occasion. He did this with a preliminary twinkle in his eye, followed by a misdeed that was effected with great panache. It was always a different trick and always a crowd-pleaser. The handler, however, was not so pleased.

Of the numerous Wheaten Terriers that have shared our home, only a small percent of them showed any interest in hunting. The majority of my Wheatens would lounge about, chin resting on unsoiled furry paws while they would benignly watch the occasional mouse that skittered across the floor. I think that my lack of interest in teaching them to hunt precipitated this behavior. (Their prospective show careers demand that I pamper

The versatile Wheaten Terrier has the intelligence and agility to excel at many different activities. Darby owned by Norma Nelson clears the bar jump at an agility trial.

and protect their coats.) I did notice, however, that a few years ago, I had taken to shooing rabbits out of my back garden. A particular young pup must have been watching me. Shortly afterwards, I became aware that when inside, she would suddenly begin to bark furiously. I would go out to look for the reason, for Wheatens are not normally noisy, yappy animals. It was a rabbit near my back garden! To this day she sounds her "bunny alerts" for me.

I have had a few Wheatens that were natural hunters. My first Wheaten Terrier, Cully, who was registered in the original studbook as #266, was a natural. She proudly presented me with her trophies over the too-few years we had her: badger, raccoon, squirrel, and her crowning achievement — a skunk!

Although his signature blond coat will go through many stages throughout adolescence, this ten-week-old shows the markings and coloration typical of a young Wheaten puppy. Owner, Marjorie and Daniel Shoemaker.

Typical of most of the terrier breeds, the Wheaten is agile. Many Wheatens prefer to launch off steps rather than go down them. They are terrier-like in their play, using their paws a bit like a cat. And they are terrier-like in their persistance. Terriers are bred to be determined, agile, and fearless in order to catch their quarry. Because of these traits, terriers will often try to get the upper hand and will continually test your resolve. Wheatens are easier-going than most of the terriers and have a basic urge to want to please their humans. However, never forget they are terriers. They do have a stubborn streak that is best handled with consistency and firmness.

The hallmark of the Soft Coated Wheaten Terrier is his lush blond coat that does not shed and is odorless. The American Wheaten carries a very abundant coat that goes through a number of stages throughout his youth, to stabilize at approximately four years of age. The puppies are born a red-brown to mahogany brown, typically with black points on ears and muzzle, sooty feet, and often a thin black stripe down the back. The puppies then gradually lose the brown coloring and black muzzle, which gives way to a rich tangerine or deep honey red at about six months of age, and lasts until about a year of age. This coat fades to a pale color during adolescence, between the ages of about 15 months to two years old. It should never be white, but will be champagne or creamy blond. The mature coloring will start showing during this time. The deeper coloring starts on the top of the dog's head and slowly travels down the neck, shoulders, and back to eventually cover the entire body.

The coat on the Wheaten begins to be more difficult to keep groomed when the puppy is about seven or eight months old. The adolescent coat is the *most* difficult of the stages. The coat seems to be comprised of a combination of textures at this age and has a great tendency to mat and snarl very quickly. Humidity in the air, and rain or snow, compound this matting problem. The coat texture, consistency, and color finally stabilize when the dog is four to four and one-half years old, and the owner is rewarded for his diligence and patience with a coat that is less dense, finer and of a single consistency that should lie in loose, shiny waves. This is a typical "proper" American coat. There are coats that diverge in texture, being less soft and fine than desired, and coats that are curlier than desired, resembling more the coat of

At about four years of age, the Wheaten Terrier's coat texture and color will stabilize and become less dense, more lustrous and hang in loose, shiny waves.

a Poodle. Both of these coats mentioned are more difficult to maintain than the "proper" coat.

The Soft Coated Wheaten Terrier is not a dog for everyone. This breed has a terrier personality with an extremely high-maintenance coat and a natural tendency to jump up and lick. He is a busy, curious, intelligent, people-oriented dog who may or may not like the other neighborhood dogs. He enjoys children and may take to being their guardian, for, like all dogs, he needs direction and purpose in his life. Being a

It's true that blondes have more fun! Although his coat is too curly according to the standard, this Soft Coated Wheaten Terrier displays the breed's tendency to jump up and give you a big kiss!

terrier, he will have his stubborn moments and test your resolve regularly. He may work at getting the upper hand. His main thought, however, is to be with you. This is a breed that prefers cool-to-cold weather and rainy days over sunny days, perhaps because of his land of origin. He is affected by hot, sunny days, looking for shade at every opportunity but willing to be with you no matter what the cost. He adores snow and will spend hours plowing his own paths. Of course, the

snow clings to his coat, abetting the matting problem. Twigs and leaves cling to his coat as well. But, if you like brushing and warm greetings in the form of "kisses," then perhaps this dog is for you.

Bikini and Green owned by Cheryl Turner Fogarty illustrate the differences between the puppy and the adult Soft Coated Wheaten Terrier.

VARIATIONS IN SOFT COATED WHEATEN TERRIERS

At this point it is important to note that there is some variation in Wheaten Terrier type here and abroad. I have judged Wheaten Terriers in England and Sweden, and have therefore had my hands on dogs from those countries as well as Finland, Norway, Denmark, and Ireland. There seems to be three general types of Wheaten. The Irish Wheaten remains truest to the original form of the breed, as depicted in earlier pictures of dogs such as Charlie Tim and Kingdom Leader. The Irish have retained a finer, much less dense coat that facilitates the dog's use in the field and makes coat maintenance easier. I am told that the fuller coats were rejected by the Irish and sent to America (and no doubt England and other countries). The ears on the Irish Wheatens are placed higher on the dog's skull, and the fold of the ears seems naturally higher as well. The temperament of the Irish

The Irish-bred Soft Coated Wheaten Terrier remains truest to the original form of the breed. A recent Irish import, Larnook Kilmaire owned by Gay Sherman Dunlap.

Wheaten varies from the America's, as these dogs tend to be more reserved and are leery of change.

The English Wheaten is a larger dog, carrying a longer neck, a longer back, and longer legs. The adults generally have a blue muzzle and blue ears, and these ears tend to be larger and lower set than the Irish and the American cousins. Constance Read was a pioneer of the Wheaten in England. Her original stock came from Holmenocks and she bred Wheatens under the Binheath prefix in the 1950s and 1960s.

Cully owned by the author is an example of what some breeders call a "poor man's Irish Wolfhound" because of his "Irish-looking" coat.

Mrs. Read bred some of her lines quite closely. As a result, there is a dominance of this type in England, as most of the Wheaten Terrier breeders in England started with dogs from her Binheath Kennels. The English dogs, while friendlier to newcomers than the Irish Wheaten, are still a bit more reserved than the American Wheaten and certainly more dignified.

Opposite: The temperament of the American-bred Wheaten Terrier has gradually become more affectionate and extroverted, winning him friends and admirers wherever he goes.

The American Wheaten has perhaps been glamorized. The fuller coat and a more "elegant terrier outline" has been sought by American breeders. The temperament of the American Wheaten has gradually become more bubbly and gregarious. The ears on the American Wheaten Terrier seem to be heavier than the Irish and more akin to the English side of their pedigrees. The American Wheaten Terrier breeders do try to retain the body type and size of their Irish forebears.

As we near the turn of the next century, Wheaten Terrier breeders are spanning oceans and continents. Irish dogs are once again being imported in order to expand our American gene pool (family tree). The English breeders and European breeders are buying American stock as well as Irish stock, and I suspect the blending of these types will produce a more uniform Wheaten Terrier throughout the world.

Irish, English and American breeders continue to work together to produce a more uniform Wheaten Terrier. Three-week-old litter bred by Marjorie and Daniel Shoemaker.

HISTORY OF THE SOFT COATED WHEATEN TERRIER

Ireland has long been noted for beauty, mystery, legendary heroes, St. Patrick, the Blarney Stone, lace, hand-blown crystal, whiskey, horses and dogs. Legend has it that the Soft Coated Wheaten Terrier is an ancient breed whose origins are lost in the mists of time. One popular theory is of the black dog who survived the sinking of a ship off the coast of Ireland and swam ashore, subsequently mating with local females to become the founding sire of a number of breeds, including the Wheaten Terrier. There are those who believe that the Terriers of Ireland descended from crossing the Irish Wolfhound with various local females. Indeed, the Wheaten Terrier has long been called the "poor man's Irish Wolfhound." There are records of wheaten-colored terriers owned by families and bred "pure" for generations. Whatever the actual origins, this medium-sized terrier with an "open" or soft wheaten colored coat has been around for nigh onto 200 years.

These versatile dogs were found on farms in counties Munster, Cork, Tipperary, Waterford, Limerick, and Kerry. They were all-purpose dogs who guarded the homestead, baby-sat the children, helped herd the cows, removed vermin from the premises, and even went bird hunting with the master. They were quick and hardy animals, intelligent with a desire to please.

The Irish are a speaking people—a story-telling people—who weave their history with colorful prose. The British are documenters. A few English books written about dogs of the British Isles, published as early as the 1880s included a chapter on "Irish Terriers" found at dog shows and fairs. The description of the dogs denoted a long-legged, medium-sized terrier wearing a variety of coat textures and colors. Some of these terriers had hard, grizzled coats, while others had "open" soft coats. The colors ranged from blue-black to pale yellow/wheaten, with gray, red, grizzled, fawn, and even harlequin color (coats of blue-black mixed with gray mottling). This description applies to three modern-day Terrier breeds originating in Ireland: the Irish Terrier, who sports a hard, red or red-wheaten coat; the Kerry Blue Terrier, whose soft, wavy coat is blue-black to slate gray; and the Soft Coated Wheaten Terrier with his soft blond coat. That these three breeds are related is

Ir. Ch. Cheerful Charlie, sired by Ch. Charlie Tim the first recorded Soft Coated Wheaten Terrier champion in Ireland.

doubtless. Which breed was the progenitor of the others is moot. There are a number of authors of dog books who have referred to the Wheaten Terrier as the original breed, including Anna Redlich, in her book *The Dogs of Ireland* published in 1949. I will only mention that the soft blond coats can be found in Irish Terrier litters, and that until the 1950s, occasional blond puppies were born into pristinely bred Kerry Blue Terrier litters.

In 1937, the Wheaten Terrier officially became a recognized breed in his native Ireland. The first recorded Irish champions were Dr. Pierse's Ch. Charlie Tim and Mr. Blake's Ch. Kingdom Leader. Both these gentlemen were instrumental in garnering the rec-

ognition of the Wheaten in Ireland. Dr. Pierse, in particular, campaigned tirelessly in attaining official recognition. In the late 1940s, Maureen Holmes, of Holmenocks Kennels, County Kildare, took up the banner and populated the present-day world with Wheaten Terriers. It is from Holmenocks that almost all the American Soft Coated Wheaten Terriers descend.

The first Soft Coated Wheaten Terrier litter whelped in the United States in 1947, bred and owned by Lydia Vogels.

Originally, Wheaten Terriers came over to America in the late 1940s. Lydia Vogels, an exhibitor of Kerry Blue Terriers, imported a male and female, whom she showed at the Westminster Dog Show and subsequently bred. Unfortunately, the breed did not "catch the fancy's eye" at that time. Cecelia O'Connor and her daughter Margaret located and imported their first Wheaten Terrier in 1957, Holmenocks Gramachree from Maureen Holmes, and had their first litter in 1962. From there, the breed gained popularity steadily. For ten years, the Wheaten Terriers were shown only in Obedience Classes and Miscellaneous Classes at AKC (American Kennel Club) Point Shows. Miscellaneous Classes are comprised of rare breeds not *officially* recognized by the AKC. These classes are proving grounds leading to AKC recognition. Meticulous Stud Book records play a key role in acceptance into the American Kennel Club. Steady growth, with a geographic distribution of the breed is the second important aspect considered. During this ten year span, approximately 1300 Soft Coated Wheaten Terriers entered the Stud Book kept by Cecelia O'Connor.

On March 17, 1973, Soft Coated Wheaten Terriers were recognized by the American Kennel Club, and on October 3, 1973, they entered their first AKC Point

Ch. Abby's Postage Dhu O'Waterford, bred by Joan Friedman and owned by the author, was the first Wheaten to gain the American championship title.

BEST OF BREED

GILBERT PHOTO

Show as a recognized breed. The first Wheaten to gain the American Championship Title was Ch. Abby's Postage Dhu O'Waterford, owned and shown by this author. He was the only dog in the United States to acquire his title the first weekend we showed. This dog was sired by Ch. Stephen Dedalus of Andover, CD, a dog bred by Cindy Gottlieb Vogels and owned by Cindy's mother, Jacqueline Gottlieb. The second Wheaten to attain his championship was Ir. Ch. Benmul Belma owned by Emily J. Holden and Carol Carlson. Belma still holds the honor of being the only Irish champion to become an American champion. The third Wheaten to become a champion was Ch. Innisfree's Annie Sullivan owned by Gay H. Sherman Dunlap. These people were dedicated to the Wheaten, and to acquiring AKC recognition, and are still active and dedicated to the breed. The three American dogs mentioned went on to become the cornerstones of the American bloodlines.

The Wheaten Terrier has continued its steady rise in popularity. In 1974, there were 467 individual Wheatens registered with the AKC, which included registration of existing dogs as foundation stock, and 95 litters that were registered. The number of litters registered (rather than individuals registered) is a truer barometer of the growth of a breed since a large percentage of pet owners never bother to register their dogs. Below is a compilation of litters registered, showing the increase in the breed's popularity.

Opposite: A pioneer of his breed, Ch. Stephan Dedalus Of Andover, CD owned by Jacqueline Gottlieb was the sire of Ch. Abby's Postage Dhu O'Waterford, the first American Wheaten champion.

Year	Litters Registered
1975	92
1976	139
1992	493
1993	502
1994	639

Ch. Innisfree's Annie Sullivan owned by Gay Sherman Dunlap.

22

STANDARD OF THE SOFT COATED WHEATEN TERRIER

The following is the official AKC Standard for the Soft Coated Wheaten Terrier with an interpretation in italics underneath. It is a written description of the ideal Wheaten Terrier and is the yardstick used by both the breeder and the dog show judge to find the dog that comes closest to that ideal. All breed standards are filled with terminology that either refers to points of the anatomy or evokes an image to those people conversant with the world of dogs.

The standard for the Wheaten Terrier varies from country to country—i.e., each country that recognizes the Wheaten Terrier has an official standard for the breed. When I judged in Sweden, I was sent the standard for the Soft Coated Wheaten Terrier in Sweden. I know it was the official standard, as it was printed in Swedish. I had it verbally translated and it sounded rather close to the Irish standard. The English standard varies in head proportions and allows for a slightly larger dog, as I recall. The American standard goes into more detail in many areas, including coat quality and presentation. The basic dog underneath the coat remains a Soft Coated Wheaten Terrier anywhere in the world.

OFFICIAL STANDARD OF THE SOFT COATED WHEATEN TERRIER

General Appearance—The Soft Coated Wheaten Terrier is a medium-sized, hardy, well balanced sporting terrier, square in outline. He is distinguished by his soft, silky, gently waving coat of warm wheaten color and his particularly steady disposition. The breed requires moderation both in structure and presentation, and any exaggerations are to be shunned. He should present the overall appearance of an alert and happy animal, graceful, strong and well coordinated.

A medium-sized dog is one whose height at the shoulder should be in the range of an average person's knee. The term "well balanced" refers to the proportions of a dog as a whole: ratio of height-to-length of body, ratio of neck length-to-height, leg length-to-height, etc. All "pieces" of the dog should be in proportion to each other, making the dog a pleasing picture to the discerning "eye" of the experienced observer. The word "sporting" refers to the Wheaten Terrier's build, as well as his agility and activity level. For his size, the Wheaten should be full of strength and energy, lithe and quick. Too much bone and too much body will slow the dog down and minimize agility, while too little bone and body draws on the dog's endurance and his ability to grapple with larger vermin.

Size, Proportion, Substance—A dog shall be 18 to 19 inches at the withers, the ideal being 18-1/2. A bitch shall be 17 to 18 inches at the withers, the ideal being 17-1/2. *Major Faults*-Dogs under 18 inches or

The Soft Coated Wheaten Terrier is a medium-sized terrier with a well-balanced, square outline. Kaler Lil' Town Flirt owned by Carol Schaltz.

Possessing a rectangular-shaped head, the Wheaten Terrier has ears that fold over and point downward. Ch. Waterford Gloria Mundi owned by Marjorie and Daniel Shoemaker.

over 19 inches; bitches under 17 inches or over 18 inches. Any deviation must be penalized according to the degree of its severity.

Square in outline. Hardy, well balanced. Dogs should weigh 35-40 pounds; bitches 30-35 pounds.

The original Wheatens were bred to a certain size and substance to accomplish the tasks for which they were bred. It is the duty of the breeder to adhere to these guidelines.

Head—Well balanced and in proportion to the body. Rectangular in appearance; moderately long. Powerful with no suggestion of coarseness.

Eyes dark reddish brown or brown, medium in size, slightly almond shaped and set fairly wide apart. Eye rims black. *Major Fault*-Anything approaching a yellow eye. *Ears* small to medium in size, breaking level with the skull and dropping slightly forward, the inside edge of the ear lying next to the cheek and pointing to the ground rather than to the eye. A hound ear or a high-breaking ear is not typical and should be *severely penalized.*

Skull flat and clean between ears. Cheekbones not prominent. Defined *stop. Muzzle* powerful and strong, well filled below the eyes. No suggestion of snipiness. Skull and foreface of equal length. Nose black and large for size of dog. *Major Fault-*Any nose color other than solid black. *Lips* tight and black. *Teeth* large, clean and white; scissors or level bite. *Major Fault* - Undershot or overshot.

The head is comprised of two areas, the skull and the muzzle. The skull is the area from the eyes to where the ears are attached. The muzzle starts just below the eyes and ends at the nose. The head,

A Wheaten puppy will go through many changes before he looks like the Soft Coated Wheaten Terrier described in the breed standard.

devoid of any hair, should fit well into a rectangle. The muzzle should not be appreciably narrower or the jaw will be weaker, especially if the head "hollows" in just below the eyes. The "plates" or bones of the skull should feel relatively flat, with no bulges or projections.

EYES: An occasional Wheaten will have large limpid eyes or eyes that are too light, both to be shunned. They should be set in the head at a slightly oblique angle to aid in peripheral vision. They should not be extremely narrow and small, such as found in some of the terrier breeds.

27

EARS: *The ears on the Wheaten Terrier can be less than perfect. The ideal ear is small and will fold slightly above the skull to fall right next to the cheek. Wheatens can have heavy ears that will have little or no lift and that will point away from the cheeks. Often these ears are also too big. Most breeders "set" the ears on their puppies at about three months of age. This is done during the "teething stage," as it seems the puppy's body is busy putting all the calcium into growing bones and teeth. The ears on these young-sters tend to lose the correct fold and sit "any old way" on their heads. Breeders put the correct fold in and glue the ears to the head for a period of time.*

SKULL: *Viewing the head in profile, the stop is that area by the eyes that connects the muzzle and skull. There should be a gentle rise over the eyes, connect-ing the two different planes of the muzzle and skull. The nose should be large and should only be black. The teeth should align properly, with the top set of front teeth slightly over the lower set, or even with the lower set.*

Neck, Topline, Body—*Neck* medium in length, clean and strong, not throaty. Carried proudly, it gradually widens, blending smoothly into the body. *Back* strong and level. *Body* compact; relatively short coupled. *Chest* is deep. *Ribs* are well sprung but without roundness. *Tail* is docked and well set on, carried gaily but never over the back.

Moderate or medium are interchangeable words used throughout the standard. We do not want to look at a dog and be aware of a very long neck or a very short neck. Either of these means that the neck length is not in proportion to the rest of the dog and is therefore exaggerated out of proportion. The Wheaten should naturally carry his head and neck high, rather than held out and down in front, unless he is trying to catch a scent of something. A "throaty" look refers to a heaviness around the throat, usually due to extra or loose skin.

The back of a dog in profile from the neck to the tail is called the "topline." This line should be level—not merely straight but level with the horizon. The body should be only long enough to balance with the length of legs. The term "short-coupled" refers to the slightly indented area between the last rib and the back leg which is called the loin. A long loin is not desirable in a Wheaten. A breeder looks for the loin space about to be three or four fingers wide, depending on the size

A judge in the show ring will make sure that your Wheaten Terrier adheres to the guidelines in the standard.

of fingers and the size of the dog. The ribs should go out from the spinal column then verge together toward the brisket (or chest) in a v-shape rather than an o-shape. A well set on tail is one that sits slightly forward on the topline so there is some rear leg behind and under the tail. The tail is correctly carried perpendicular to the back.

Forequarters—*Shoulders* well laid back, clean and smooth; well knit. *Forelegs* straight and well boned. All *dewclaws* should be removed. *Feet* are round and compact with good depth of pad. *Pads* black. *Nails* dark.

The most complex part of a dog, the forequarters are an essential part of the running gear of a dog. Breeders want the shoulders placed at a 45-degree angle from the perpendicular and to be blended so well into the body they are difficult to discern. This placement generally means that the connecting bones will also be placed properly to create a long-reaching stride with the front legs. The front legs and feet should look straight from any viewpoint. Dewclaws are the sixth toe that has evolved upwards on the dog's lower inside leg. Cats have them as well and use them almost like the opposable thumb when catching and holding on to prey. I would guess they got their name because they were the height to catch

Considered the driving gear of your dog, the hindquarters of your Wheaten Terrier should be muscular and well-developed.

the dew on grass. These appendages are not necessary to the dog and often can catch on things or get torn or cut off by accident. Breeders remove them at the same time the tails are docked.

Hindquarters—*Hind legs* well developed with well bent *stifles* turning neither in nor out; *hocks* well let down and parallel to each other. All *dewclaws* should be removed. The presence of dewclaws on the hind legs should be *penalized. Feet* are round and compact with good depth of pad. *Pads* black. *Nails* dark.

The driving gear of the dog, the hindquarters are the complement of the forequarters. Here again, the angles of the bones come into play so they allow the rear legs to reach forward and push the dog onward with impulsion.

Coat—A distinguishing characteristic of the breed which sets the dog apart from all other terriers. An abundant single coat covering the entire body, legs and head; coat on the latter falls forward to shade the eyes. Texture soft and silky with a gentle wave. In both puppies and adolescents, the mature wavy coat is generally not yet evident. *Major Faults* -Woolly or harsh, crisp or cottony, curly or standaway coat; in the adult, a straight coat is also objectionable.

Presentation-For show purposes, the Wheaten is presented to show a terrier outline, but coat must be of sufficient length to flow when the dog is in motion. The coat must never be clipped or plucked. Sharp contrasts or stylizations must be avoided. Head coat should be blended to present a rectangular outline. Eyes should be indicated but never fully exposed. Ears should be relieved of fringe, but not taken down to the leather. Sufficient coat must be left on skull, cheeks, neck and tail to balance the proper length of body coat. *Dogs that are overly trimmed shall be severely penalized.*

Because our American Wheaten coats are much thicker than the original Irish ancestors', we breeders have had to contend with coats that are woolly, cottony, too curly, too straight, and even too thick. All these coat qualities have confused breeders and judges alike, which resulted in descriptions of the proper coat, as well as the noticeable changes in coat color and texture, as the dog matures.

We breeders do not want a "Kerry Blond" Terrier, but a dog that, while trimmed to show the terrier outline, carries some coat length. Like the dog, the trim should also be moderate.

Color—Any shade of wheaten. Upon close examination, occasional red, white or black guard hairs may be found. However, the overall coloring must be clearly wheaten with no evidence of any other color

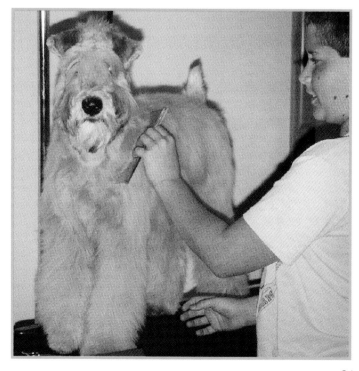

The characteristic that sets the Wheaten apart from other terriers is his wheaten-colored, single coat. Owners, the Donahue family.

except on ears and muzzle where blue-gray shading is sometimes present. *Major Fault*-Any color save wheaten.

Puppies and Adolescents-Puppies under a year may carry deeper coloring and occasional black tipping. The adolescent, under two years, is often quite light in color, but must never be white or carry gray other than on ears and muzzle. However, by two years of age, the proper wheaten color should be obvious.

The Wheaten Terrier should be a blond dog. Puppies can be a deep strawberry blond; adolescents can be platinum blond; adults should be a definite blond—

The Soft Coated Wheaten Terrier's gait should be free, graceful and lively, making him appear to "float" effortlessly.

an intermingling of red and white hairs with gold hairs—and only occasional black guard hairs. The Wheaten Terrier should never look sooty or dirty but look clear blond and never white.

Gait—Gait is free, graceful and lively with good reach in front and strong drive behind. Front and rear feet turn neither in nor out. Dogs who fail to keep their tails erect when moving should be *severely penalized.*

This is the ideal result of the forequarters and hindquarters being properly placed on a properly-shaped body. The dog should "float" effortlessly along in a smooth, efficient, ground-covering gait. Viewed from the side, the topline should remain level and should not sway, roll, or bounce. The front legs should reach easily beyond the nose before touching the ground and the rear legs should push off the ground well behind the tail. Viewing the front of a moving dog,

Have no fear, your Wheatie's here! Whether awake or asleep, your Wheaten Terrier offers your whole family protection and love. Owners, the Donahue family.

there should be no perceptible shifting of weight from one side to another, no elbows popping out, no glimpse of the pads of the front feet, nor evidence of the knee as a front leg reaches forward and contacts the ground. The legs should remain relatively straight looking, with no bowed or crooked lines. Viewed from the rear, the rear legs should move in a relatively straight manner. They should not look bowed out, crooked or "cow-hocked" where the hocks point in-ward toward each other and the toes point out.

Temperament—The Wheaten is a happy, steady dog and shows himself gaily with an air of self-confidence. He is alert and exhibits interest in his surroundings; exhibits less aggressiveness than is sometimes encouraged in other terriers. *Major Fault-*Timid or overly aggressive dogs.

Whereas males can be more aggressive with each other than females, most Wheatens tend to be friendly and will stand their ground or walk up to another dog. The females tend to be less interested in other dogs while in the show ring, as they are fixed on the tidbits offered by the handler. The breed should exhibit some pleasure in showing at dog shows. Often inexperi-enced pups look at the judge with an eye to jumping up and greeting them. There should never be any aggression shown toward a judge.

Approved February 12, 1983
Reformatted July 20, 1989

SELECTING YOUR SOFT COATED WHEATEN TERRIER

The Wheaten Terrier is not the right breed for everyone. The grooming, the attention he craves, and his terrier temperament makes this breed less than ideal for some people. However, he is a wonderful companion, possessing style, panache, and that "joie de vivre" particular to the terrier breeds.

Once you have decided that your life would not be complete until you live with a Soft Coated Wheaten Terrier, there are two excellent ways to find a reliable breeder of quality animals. Locate the all-breed Kennel Club in your area, and ask for the names of exhibitor/breeders of Wheaten Terriers or contact your national kennel club, such as the American Kennel Club, Canadian Kennel Club or the Kennel Club of Great Britan and ask for the name of the secretary of the Soft Coated Wheaten Terrier Clubs.

How can you resist these adorable faces? The decision to fall in love with a Wheaten pup is an easy one, but make sure you carefully consider the responsibilities of pet ownership before taking one home.

The national kennel club will also be able to give you the names of the all-breed kennel clubs in your area. You may also procure the standard for the Soft Coated Wheaten Terrier. It is by this written description of the ideal Wheaten Terrier that breeders strive to produce the perfect Wheaten and dog show judges try to find the perfect Wheaten in the conformation ring.

This big ball of Wheaten fluff may look like a teddy bear, but this puppy is a living creature that requires lots of time, care and attention from his owner.

In the United States, there are local kennel clubs in every area of the country. They are comprised of a regional membership of the "doggy set;" breeders, exhibitors, and judges. These clubs are always "geographically" named — for a city, a county, or a region. Mile-High Kennel Club is located in the Denver, Colorado area; Boardwalk Kennel Club is located in Atlantic City, New Jersey; Mississippi Valley KC is located in St. Louis, Missouri; and Mason-Dixon KC is in Maryland, situated near that famous line. There are hundreds of kennel clubs affiliated with the American Kennel Club (AKC) liberally sprinkled all over the country. These clubs hold an AKC "point show" annually or biannually. Point shows are those shows put on through the auspices of the AKC, where any recognized breed may be entered to compete for points toward championship status. Your local newspaper will often list an upcoming AKC dog show in the "Weekend" or the "Events" section. Some kennel clubs have their own phone number and are listed in the phone book.

Your goal is to get in touch with breeders/exhibitors who are working to improve the breed, according to the written standard (competition keeps people on their toes). These breeders have a long-range goal

that encompasses not only beauty but physical and mental soundness. They look ahead, searching for sounder dogs. Each litter represents a stepping stone, a building block of their foundation, and a breeder who exhibits at Point shows wants a sound foundation upon which to continue building. There is little or no money to be made, as breeders will expend vast sums of money checking their breeding stock for health and inheritable diseases as well as entering and showing at dog shows. These breeders know their dogs and raise their puppies with great care and love. A lot has been put into a litter from a breeder/exhibitor. They will have knowledge of the parents and grandparents and will understand the individual personalities of the pups in a litter. Most breeders do not let their pups go before ten weeks of age and will hold on to several pups for a number of months, hoping to keep the best.

Conscientious Soft Coated Wheaten Terrier breeders will be concerned with working to improve the breed and lessen the chances of any future health problems.

Dogs and children can be great friends, but be sure to educate your child on the proper care and handling of a Soft Coated Wheaten Terrier before leaving the two unsupervised.

When you contact a breeder, you will find that there is a network of breeders. If one breeder has no pups at this time, he or she will give you the name of breeders to call who may have a litter, or who may know of a litter. When you have located a breeder who has a puppy for sale, you will find that the breeder will ask questions about your situation in regard to owning a dog. These questions pertain to your family and work and they will give the breeder a frame of reference and allow him or her to assess your lifestyle. Do you work away from the home? Do you have a fenced yard? Do you have children? These and other questions help the breeder to evaluate your situation and get to know you. After all, most breeders feel rather like an adoption agency. They know their dogs and will guide you as to which temperament or which sex would best fit in your household.

There is a difference between the two sexes. The Wheaten male is more constant and loving. He tends

Raising dogs from puppyhood, especially Wheaten Terriers, requires canine knowledge, consistence and lots of patience! Callie owned by Marjorie and Daniel Shoemaker.

to be calmer than the female and more loyal to the family. He is more easily trained, as he wants to please you, although he can also be stubborn. As an added treat, he has a sense of humor. Due to the fact that males are instinctively territorial, they tend to be more protective of their humans.

The female of the species can work a room better than Pearl Mesta. She is busy, gregarious, and down-right flirtatious. Nothing goes unnoticed. The female epitomizes the iron paw in the velvet glove. She is very clever at eventually having the household re-volve around her personal agenda. She can some-times be spiteful if she feels she was ignored or left behind, leaving a little "present" for you or chewing your best throw pillow. Be warned—females are harder to procure, as breeders are stingy with them. Females, more than males, represent the next generation in their breeding program. It is much easier for breeders to keep multiple females than to keep multiple males. But if I were put into a position of having only one Wheaten, I would definitely choose a male. The male bonds more closely with his clan. The final decision, however, rests with the prospective owners.

The Wheaten's ability to read your moods gives you the feeling that the breed is intuitive and, at times, even telepathic. As mentioned, Wheatens are keen observers of humans and will react instinctively to your feelings. Still, it must be remembered that these furry creatures are dogs, and terriers to boot. They look like stuffed toys, especially as puppies, which makes your job as taskmaster more difficult. Raising dogs, especially Wheaten Terriers from puppyhood, requires some knowledge of canine behavior, consistent training, and patience. Wheatens are smart—sometimes too smart.

HAVE YOU CONSIDERED AN ADULT?

Some people do not have the time or the inclination to go through the training of a puppy and are willing to miss that "cute puppy" stage. They prefer an older Wheaten whose rough edges have been smoothed to a civilized polish. Most Wheaten breeders have their youngsters in the home, raising the puppies as part of the family. Getting an older dog from an exhibitor/breeder has proven satisfactory for a number of reasons. This dog comes with basic house manners. He will be crate trained, housebroken, trained to the leash, and will understand a number of words, including "no, "come," and "outside." He will probably be past the chewing stage, and he will have table manners — grooming table, that is. It may well be a dog who already has acquired his AKC Championship and who has had puppies, thereby contributing to the breeder's gene pool. I feel that dogs who have had a

If you do not have the time or inclination to train a puppy, consider adopting an adult Soft Coated Wheaten Terrier.

few litters deserve to reign supreme, so to speak, as a single dog in a home rather than remain one of many dogs.

I will mention that there are two problems to deal with when placing an older dog. I do not place an older Wheaten in a home that is vacated daily for work and/or school. My dogs have never been alone for any length of time, for even if we are gone, they have the company of each other and two cats. For this home, I strongly recommend a puppy who has not developed a routine yet. Being creatures very reliant on routine, adult dogs are slower than puppies to adapt to a new daily regimen. The second problem, while not insurmountable, requires a good deal of patience - namely, a home with no fencing where the dog will be walked. Put a leash on my dogs and they parade around excitedly, ready to go into the show ring. They have no idea that they are on leash to eliminate, as they are used to being let out the door into a fenced area. (Collars, no matter how soft, are shunned by breeders, as they will damage the coat, leaving an unsightly ring around the neck. This is not desirable in the show ring.)

Contrary to popular belief, I have never seen a problem with older dogs not bonding with their new family. This is a myth, totally unfounded, in my experience. I admit it makes a great movie plot, but such utter devotion in any dog, especially this breed, is extremely rare. I see dogs bonding with the professional handlers at the dog shows. These handlers would not be able to show successfully if the dogs did not bond to them in some way. I have placed a number of adults who have bonded and adjusted to their new clan with great success. In fact, I cannot recall any failures.

I placed a seven-year-old Wheaten female with my parents. Amber was special to us but she needed to be "Queen." A year later I made my first visit back home since we sent Amber. She came to the door barking when I knocked. I started talking to her through the door and the sound of her voice left no doubt she remembered me. When Mother opened the door, Amber threw herself on me, danced, leapt, talked, and in general turned herself inside out. We went into the living room, Amber escorted me to my chair and gave me a few wet kisses, then promptly trotted over to my mother and sat down at her feet, panting from her exertions and excitement. Mother and I talked for a few minutes, and I watched Amber, who had not budged from my mother's leg. My mother somehow mustered the courage to suggest that Amber obviously loved us so much that perhaps she should return with me. I believe I saw a tear in my mother's eye. My mother could not see Amber's face and "body language" from her position. Amber was leaning hard against my mother's leg and staring directly at me, every inch of her radiating her preference to stay. I do believe Amber was worried that I had come to take her back home with me.

Dogs, like humans, form bonds throughout their lifetimes. Both are capable of infinite numbers of relationships while still remembering past relationships. I have had puppies leave my house at nine and

Spaying or neutering your Wheaten will help to lessen your dog's risk of developing serious health problems later in life. Owners, Marjorie and Daniel Shoemaker.

ten weeks of age who remember me with great fondness years later. Dogs that I have "loaned" out remember the people who baby-sat them and delight in seeing them. Adult Wheaten Terriers will readily form relationships with new friends. It is part and parcel with the Wheaten Terrier credo, "When I am not with the ones I love, I love the ones I am with."

PAPERWORK

Wheaten breeders sell their dogs to homes with one of two sales contracts. The "show" contract is for a promising-looking puppy, and the owner is required to show the dog to his AKC Championship prior to breeding the dog. The dog show is, after all, the breeder's proving ground. If the dog is good enough to breed, the dog should prove his worth in the show ring. The "pet" contract is for a puppy going strictly as a companion and pet, and the owner will have the animal neutered before the breeder signs over the AKC registration papers.

The neutered Wheaten makes a much better pet. An unspayed female goes through a three-week heat cycle twice in a year, attracting every male dog within a four mile radius, staining carpets and upholstery, and in general acting rather high-strung. An unneutered male is more territorial, often lifting his leg within the home to "mark" or define his territory, and more aggressive, tending to be overprotective. Both male and female Wheaten Terriers who have been neutered become calmer individuals and have even less interest in straying.

Wheatens are basically "home-bodies," as their duty is to protect the home from intruders such as vermin. This is unlike the hounds and sporting dog breeds that were bred to forage great distances to hunt stag, fox, birds, etc. Terriers stray from home if they are busy chasing off varmints, if they are bereft of companionship, or if their "hormones are raging," so to speak. By nature, both the male and the female will seek out a mate. Neutering a dog will eliminate this need to go looking for a mate. Neutering will also minimize potential health problems. Males that are not used at stud will often develop prostate problems, and females will likely develop uterine or mammary problems. Lastly, many cities and towns are charging "premium" annual dog license fees for unneutered dogs of both sexes. There are many valid reasons to neuter your pet, and only one reason not to.

Your Wheaten puppy will begin to form bonds with humans while he is still at the breeders and will continue to develop relationships with people throughout his lifetime.

A purebred dog's pedigree will list his ancestor's names as well as any titles they might have earned. Callie owned by Marjorie and Daniel Shoemaker competes in the show ring.

When you reach the point of purchasing the pup or adult, your breeder will furnish you with a packet of information, that should include health history and a record of the dog's inoculations, and handbook on raising a Wheaten Terrier that should include a discussion on crate training and a section on grooming and recommended grooming tools, a contract, and a pedigree. The pedigree is the family tree of your dog. It will list on the top half your puppy's sire (father), followed by the sire's parents, grandparents, great-grandparents, etc.; on the bottom half, your puppy's dam (mother), her parents, grandparents, and so on. Most, if not all, of your puppy's ancestors will have a "Ch." in front of the registered name. This is the abbreviation for champion. Ir. Ch. is the abbreviation of Irish champion. AmCan. Ch. before the name means American and Canadian Champion, a dual title. ROM after the dog's name stands for Register of Merit, a title indicating that this Wheaten has produced a number of dogs that became champions, and was recognized for this accomplishment by the Soft Coated Wheaten Terrier Club of America (SCWTCA).

Other letters after a dog's name indicate obedience titles or working titles gained at dog shows: CD stands for Companion Dog, CDX is Companion Dog Excellent, and UD is Utility Dog. TD is Tracking Dog, TDX Tracking Dog Excellent. There are agility titles and Canine Good Citizen titles, Field Trial titles, Therapy Dog titles, and more that are recognized.

If you are buying a puppy as a companion and family pet, the breeder will withhold the AKC registration papers, or what we call the blue slip. This blue slip is your dog's official entry into permanent AKC stud book registry and has information on it, such as names of the sire and dam, their registration numbers, their obedience and conformation titles, the breeder's name, the date of the puppy's birth, and the puppy's identification number. This blue slip is not a necessity for any dog that will not be bred. Many people who buy pets never bother to register their Wheaten. After all, they have the dog's pedigree in hand.

Should you wish in the future to enter your Wheaten Terrier in AKC obedience trials, and you never bothered to register him, you can easily apply to the AKC for an ILP (Indefinite Listing Privilege). An ILP number is used for those breeds of dogs not yet recognized by the AKC, and for purebred dogs obtained either as pets or through perhaps the auspices of a local animal shelter, where no papers are turned over. This is a relatively simple process, requiring you to fill out the form they sent you and usually requiring a photo of the dog and a copy of the dog's pedigree, if you have it. Your dog will be eligible to compete for most of the titles with the exception of champion, and of course, ROM.

Time spent with littermates is a critical part of canine socialization. Twelve-week-old pups owned by Marjorie and Daniel Shoemaker.

SOCIALIZATION

The exhibitor/breeder devotes himself to a litter from prior to whelping until the puppies leave the house. He spends innumerable hours overseeing, feeding, cleaning and, in general, watching puppies develop from defenseless, palm-sized life forms that are blind and deaf their first few weeks into furry rapscallions who are full of energy and curiosity. They are bubbling over with enthusiasm one minute and sound asleep the next minute. Every new thing a puppy comes upon has to pass the "taste test." Puppies are like children. They must have constant supervision or be contained in a safe environment such as a puppy pen or crate.

The breeder handles the puppies from birth, weighing them daily the first three or four weeks and checking them over briefly. Nails are trimmed weekly from birth. They are under constant scrutiny and supervision — partly for the sheer joy and fascination they bring and partly for the search for that perfect show puppy. Every puppy is treated as that potential "super puppy."

Little personalities start to emerge at three weeks of age. This is when puppies become individuals. They are up on their feet, albeit a bit wobbly at first. As they gain strength and muscle tone, their little outlines start to take shape. This is also about the time the dam gets a bit bored with the business of motherhood. She is getting cabin fever.

By the fourth week, the puppies have been able to see and hear for a week. They have become very aware of their surroundings. Their baby teeth are

A Wheaten that was properly socialized when young will get along famously with other dogs — especially other Wheatens! Owners, the Donahue family.

Due to the Wheaten's boundless energy and enthusiasm, there is always plenty of pandemonium where puppies are found!

budding, giving mother warning of the fine crop of "needles" that will soon fill their mouths. The pups are beginning on solid food, and are ready to learn about the world.

It is time to move them from their whelping area that was in a warm and quiet part of the house. They will now be put in the "busiest" room in the house, to accustom them to changes, and noises (such as TV, radio, telephone) and hubbub of all kinds. They are regularly admired and played with and are allowed daily romps around the room with supervision, of course.

At four weeks, the puppies are started on the grooming table. They are posed, encouraged, and trimmed just a bit, at first. Each session on the grooming table is expanded, and they will be brushed and combed and trimmed regularly.

By eight weeks, these puppies are very "humanized" and are generally on a completely solid food diet. (Some breeders allow the dams to decide when they no longer wish to nurse. The dams will wean the puppies naturally.) Eight weeks is also that time I refer to as the "terrible two's in pups." Somewhere between seven and one-half weeks and eight and one-half weeks, there is pandemonium and chaos in the litter. The pups are all grappling for leader position, I think. There are terribly noisy, yappy discussions and fights that evolve during play. There are pitiful yelps as little needle teeth are chewing on a littermate's ear or lip.

A Wheaten Terrier that has received a generous amount of love and understanding will return that love to his family a hundred times over.

I am always relieved when things settle down again the following week, and some sense of order returns. It follows immediately that the pups get a sense of cleanliness and they begin to await my morning arrival so they may go outside to relieve themselves. It is the dawn of "puppy civilization," and the time nears for the little ones to move on toward their new destinations.

CARE OF YOUR SOFT COATED WHEATEN TERRIER

ADVANCE PREPARATION

Prior to bringing your new Wheaten home, there are a few things you must do. You must acquire a crate (never call it a cage), dog food, safe toys, and a collar and leash. You should line up a veterinarian and, if you plan to have your dog professionally groomed, a reputable grooming establishment. If you are you planning to walk your dog, do you have a secured fenced area or planning to install one? Where will this new family member sleep?

Before your Softie arrives at his new home, be sure to purchase the basic items he'll need and have a supply of the food he's been eating on hand.

Talk to your breeder about crates, food, toys and collars. The crate will be your dog's private bedroom and traveling suite. Your breeder can tell you what neck size to look for in collars. He will most likely steer you to the preferred rolled leather collar or the round (not flat) braided nylon collar, for minimal coat damage. If you plan to buy a collar that will be kept on the dog at all times, it is safer to buy a buckle collar that is worn loosely around the neck. If you walk the dog

Getting accustomed to a new environment may be difficult for a puppy. Care, kindness, and encouragement will make him feel secure and help him to become a well-adjusted adult.

with that collar, buckle it a hole tighter so the dog can't back out of the collar should he suddenly decide to chase a squirrel or cat, or use a choke collar for the walks. A choke collar is a metal chain with a ring on each end, although you can locate rolled leather and round braided nylon choke collars that are gentler on the neck coat.

The toys that Wheatens enjoy are the "fake sheepskin" toys that come in various shapes and often come equipped with a squeaker. The latex squeaky toys, especially the ones that look like porcupines, fascinate the puppies. Gumabones® are a big hit with puppies, as they are softer versions of the Nylabones®, which are great for adults. I will give the dogs an occasional cow hoof or pig's ear as a treat. I tend to

49

Always be sure to feed age-appropriate food designed to meet the nutritional needs of your puppy, adult, or senior dog.

stay away from the rawhide bones, especially smaller sized ones, with dogs over six months of age. The rawhide gets soft with chewing, and the dog tries to swallow it, often choking on it. However molded rawhide, called Roar-Hide®, is safe and eagerly accepted by Wheatens.

FEEDING

Your breeder will tell you the brand of dog food and the amounts to be fed, although generally, two cups of food is daily ration for the breed. You will be wise to start with the same food to minimize the effects of the new environment your new Wheaten has to deal with. If you wish to change to another brand, you may do so, but it is recommended you do so gradually, over a week's time, mixing the

Provide your Wheaten Terrier with cool, clean water at all times. Owners, Marjorie and Daniel Shoemaker.

original brand of food with the new brand. Wheatens tend to have sensitive stomachs, and, as dried foods differ not only in ingredients but in how they are produced, an abrupt change will possibly cause soft or runny stool.

All breeders feed a dry dog food (or kibble) and many Wheaten breeders use a lamb and rice diet, as some Wheatens have allergic reactions to beef, wheat, corn, and even chicken. Both lamb and rice are hypo-allergenic foods. This kibble is fed with water added. Some breeders, like myself, will add a very small amount of plain yogurt (or cottage cheese) and ground meat, and add water to make a light gravy. This is not necessary, as a good brand of kibble is perfectly balanced nutrition for your dog. I feel that the sauce makes this food a bit more enticing. The dried food is best for your dog and should be 90 to 95 percent of your dog's diet.

Avoid giving your Wheaten human junk food. Chocolate especially and other candy is not meant for dogs. The same goes for potato chips, cheese doodles, and such. If you wish, you may give him leftovers from your meals, consisting of small amounts of meats and vegetables. Make sure young children are not feeding your dog. Some foods, especially junk foods or dessert foods, may cause your Wheaten to get sick. It is not advisable to give your dog cooked meat bones. Cooked bones have minimal food value and often become brittle, splintering when chewed upon. These splinters can cause serious damage when swallowed. Uncooked bones will not tend to splinter, although it is unwise to ever give your dog chicken bones or pork bones. If you wish to give your Wheaten a bone, Nylabones® are the safest.

Wheaten males can be picky eaters. This is first noticed in pups that are 14 or 15 weeks old. I suspect this might be due to cutting teeth. I tend to ignore the fact that a dog doesn't always finish a meal. (Remember that the wild relatives of the dog—the wolf, coyote, and fox all live day to day - gorging then fasting until they catch their next meal.) The canine

Make sure you give your Wheaten puppy the proper nutrients he requires for growth or he may go looking for them on his own!

digestive system will not be damaged by missing a meal or two. The *worst* thing you can do with a picky eater is to take notice and try changing foods or adding enticing goodies to the meal. These dogs are smart enough to realize that a great game is afoot! They will lead you a merry chase, shopping and cooking for them. No matter what you feed or what you add, I can almost guarantee that the dog will tire of it in two weeks, and you will once again be trying to find something that will appeal to them. Just stick to one dog food brand and minimize your enticing additives, thereby saving yourself a great deal of frustration. If he does not finish two or three meals in a row, cut back a bit on the amount you feed. A dog can get into the habit of always leaving something in the bowl. When he finishes his meal a few times, increase the amount again and see if he will finish that meal. Summer heat will curtail your dog's activity level and his appetite. Teething will do the same, as will experiencing seasons or heat (females) or a change in environment. Eventually, the dog's eating habits will stabilize. Please have the patience to see it through with a minimum of fuss made.

Physical activity benefits your Wheaten's mental and emotional health, as well as his body.

EXERCISE

Wheaten youngsters require more exercise than adults. Like children, they are equipped with boundless energy. The more exercise a youngster gets the less mischief he is likely to look for and the better and the longer he will sleep at night.

Take your Wheaten on walks, teach him to chase a ball or a Frisbee. Play with him and his toys. If you have children, they will match the puppy's energy level.

Children and puppies are drawn to each other. Both the child and the puppy recognize their "simpatico." If your children are under the age of ten, playtime should *always* be supervised, for two reasons. Proper housebreaking requires alert adult eyes to catch the puppy in the act of eliminating indoors and immediate correction, and playing should never get out of hand or hurtful. Puppies and dogs, if they get accidentally startled or hurt, react instinctively and quickly. They yelp, turn on the "culprit," and snap at him or her—all in the blink of an eye. Such an experience can have negative reactions. It could frighten a child, or worse, hurt a child. It could discourage a puppy from the children in the future, or it could lead to worse behavior if not nipped in the bud. Adults must supervise as to what play is allowable and nonthreatening to both child and puppy. The adult should also be watching to see if the puppy is getting tired. If the pup is allowed to retreat and take a nap, he will be all the more refreshed and eager for the next playtime.

When your Wheaten is six months old, he will be eligible to be enrolled in obedience classes. These classes are generally ten weeks of one-hour sessions, requiring daily practice of 20 to 30 minutes duration. This is an excellent way to burn excess energy.

Learning basic obedience will allow your Wheaten Terrier to expend his energy on productive activities. Casey O'Malley practices heeling with owner Carol Shaltz.

GROOMING YOUR SOFT COATED WHEATEN TERRIER

Any breed of dog requires good grooming practices. Even shorthaired breeds will benefit from brushing and combing and occasional bathing. Grooming will remove dead hair and debris, and in double-coated breeds, minimize the shedding hair that will rub off on clothes, carpeting, and furniture. Grooming allows you to check for parasites, cuts, or skin conditions that might require attention. It allows you to devote undivided attention to your dog, and can be a pleasurable experience for both of you.

Your Wheaten puppy has been groomed and has had rudimentary lessons on the grooming table. Pa-

Regular grooming is an excellent way to minimize matting and to detect any skin or coat problems your dog may have.

tience and repetition will teach your Wheaten to stand relatively still while you groom him. A Wheaten puppy coat is very easy to care for and needs much less attention than an adult coat. However, it is very important to brush and comb your puppy at least once a week to instill good grooming manners for the longer sessions that are to come. You, or the future groomer, will be very grateful that you did.

If you plan to have your Wheaten professionally groomed, you will find most grooming parlors will be familiar with Wheaten Terriers and how to trim them. Nail cutting is generally done by the groomer, but you should ask about removing hair from the ear canal. Generally, that will be included but is not required of many breeds. The groomer might need a reminder from you as you hand your dog over for his beauty appointment.

A word of warning! There are some grooming establishments that will, as a matter of course, give tranquilizers or sedatives to the dogs they are grooming, while some groomers will tranquilize only those dogs they deem "troublesome." I hasten to recommend you locate a groomer that does *not* give any drugs to dogs. A Wheaten Terrier's metabolism is such that he can overreact to these substances, taking as long as two days to return to normal.

If you plan to do the grooming and trimming yourself, your breeder will give you pointers and lessons. Trimming your Wheaten will allow him to look much more stylish, and will facilitate the coat maintenance. The Soft Coated Wheaten Terrier Club of America, Inc. has an Owner's Manual that devotes an entire chapter to trimming, taking you through the process step by step. There is also a grooming chart available from this club, and there are several well-done videos available. Practical application is your best learning tool. Just dig in and DO IT! If you make a mistake — and you will — don't worry! The hair will grow back. It is most forgiving, like its owner.

Below, I have listed the grooming equipment necessary. If you plan to have your dog professionally groomed, you will need only the first two items on the list:

GREYHOUND COMB: Made in Belgium, this 7-inch comb has narrower teeth than other combs, enabling it to get through long thick coats. I have not found any other comb to work.

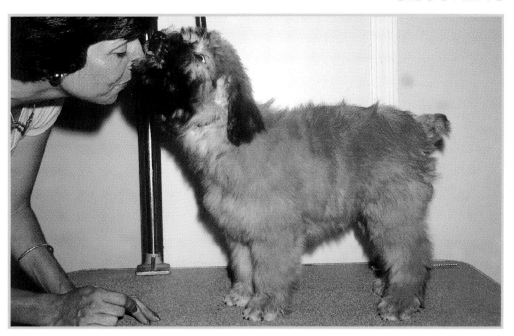

If you accustom your Wheaten puppy to grooming procedures when he is young, he will come to consider it a pleasurable experience.

MEDIUM-SIZE SLICKER BRUSH: A brush with a rectangular head that is filled with many small pins set into the head at an angle. I prefer a medium-soft slicker brush.

MAT RAKE or mat splitter: There are a variety of these tools available. I prefer a rake that will break up the mat not slice through it, as the mat splitter will.

TOENAIL CLIPPERS: Again there are different types; scissor action and guillotine action. It is best to try holding them and working them to see which type you prefer.

TWEEZERS or hemostat: To pull hair out of ear canals.

SCISSORS: I recommend you get a decent pair of straight-edge hair scissors that will be used only for hair. Do not cut paper, or even thread, with these scissors.

THINNING SHEARS: If you plan to trim your Wheaten yourself, invest in a decent pair of thinning shears. There are two types of thinning shears: single-edged with one blade straight and one blade "toothed," and double-edged, where both blades are "toothed." I prefer the single-edged shears, as the pattern of coat removal is less noticeable.

GROOMING TABLE: Is a table approximately 24" by 30" that has a rubber top upon which the dog will stand while being preened. It has folding legs and can easily be made, rather than bought.

GROOMING ARM AND GROOMING NOOSE: A metal pole that clamps onto the grooming table, upon which you attach the grooming noose. While the dog is on the table, the dog's head will be contained by the grooming noose. This tool is used as a restraint so the dog will not jump off the table.

BRUSHING AND COMBING

By the age of five months, the average coat of the Wheaten Terrier will require "layer grooming." This term refers to the process of brushing and combing the coat, an inch or two of coat at a time, and *from the*

skin. This is most important. I have had Wheaten Terriers brought to me that looked beautifully groomed but had heavy matting at the skin. This is why I only can recommend the Greyhound comb and why we layer groom! I start at the underline (chest and tummy area) and work up.

First I "backbrush" the entire dog (brush against the lie of the coat). Backbrushing will help to locate and "loosen" or spread any coat that is starting to mat. Then I go to the area I want to work. If it is a front leg, I backbrush the entire leg, more carefully this time, working from the elbow and down to the toes. Then,

Backbrushing your Wheaten Terrier's coat will help spread the coat and loosen any mats. Owners, Marjorie and Daniel Shoemaker.

starting at the toes, I brush an inch of coat down again and from the skin. I always follow this by combing that section. The comb will double-check your work. Bring the next layer of coat down and brush firmly down, following with the comb. Continue all the way up the front leg, brushing then combing each layer. When you are finished with the leg, comb from top to bottom all the way around the leg. This is your last double-check of this area. Move on to perhaps the back leg, and repeat the general backbrush and the more detailed backbrush of that area. Then brush one inch of the hair at toes, comb that inch, go to the next inch up the back leg and repeat until you have reached the top of the dog's back. The next area would be the body, starting with the chest. I hold the balance of the coat out of the way of my "layering" with my other arm. Work your way up the sides, then to the neck and top of the back. The beard and the forelock (hair falling over the eyes) can be broken into areas as well. Brush the mustache hairs (on the side of the muzzle back toward the ears) then taking a bit at a time, brush and comb forward. The same can be done with the goatee or hair on the chin. Wheatens hate this part, however. I find that I must hold part of the beard in one hand, while I groom another part, or they will play "Duck the

An example of parting the coat into layers while grooming a Soft Coated Wheaten Terrier's front leg.

Brush." The areas that require the most diligence are the "tops" of the legs, where they are attached to the body, and the chest. The beard will also require extra attention because they all love to rub their beards against your good sofa after a meal.

Worth Repeating: Always follow the brushing of each layer with combing. Be sure you are combing from the skin. The final combing of the whole section (i.e., leg, body, neck, etc.) will "rake" the coat, removing those few hairs that will be tomorrow's mat. Do not be too gentle. You must make sure to get the comb all the way to the skin.

If you are faithful in your grooming obligations, you can keep the coat in good condition with about 45 to 60 minutes of work twice a week. The difficult ages are 16 months of age through about 28 months of age, when the Wheaten has his cottony adolescent coat. It gets a bit easier after that, and then gets easier again at about four years of age. This is his true adult coat and it will be less dense and improved in quality.

BATHING

I recommend bathing your Wheaten every three or four weeks if you plan to groom him yourself. Some Wheaten Terriers have an "oilier" skin and coat that

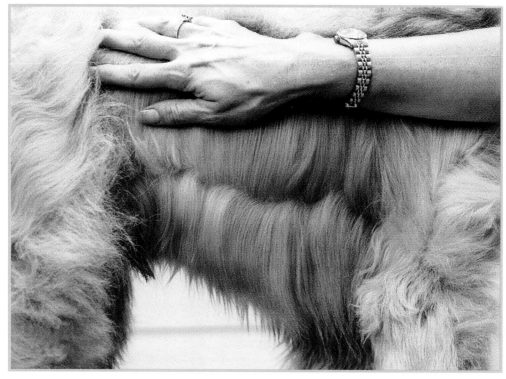

To prevent heavy matting in the undercoat, Wheaten Terriers should be layer groomed to ensure that all of the coat is thoroughly brushed.

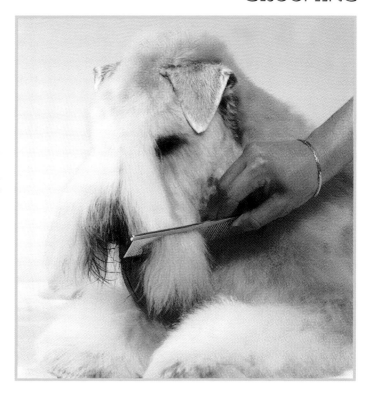

Pay extra attention to cleaning and combing your Wheaten's beard, as it can get dirty and matted — especially at feeding time.

will make grooming more difficult by the end of the second week. Your Wheaten won't have any "doggy odor," as the breed is odorless, but you will be able to tell when the coat gets hard to groom — the comb drags through the coat, and ten minutes after being freshly groomed, the coat will look "clumpy" again. These individuals will do well being bathed every two weeks. It should not damage or dry out the coat, unless you are using a shampoo that is too harsh, or blowing the coat with a hot dryer. In the summertime, I don't bother to blow dry at all unless the dog is going to a show; I just let them dry outdoors.

Before bathing your dog, make sure you have thoroughly groomed him and removed all the mats! This is very important. Small mats that go into the bath come out much larger, full of soap, and very difficult to break apart. Save yourself a lot of work by grooming before the bath. Use a mild soap, and, if you wish, a detangler rinse that will minimize future mats by putting a bit of oil back into the coat. You may find you will be bathing more often with use of the rinse, in which case try shampooing but not using the cream rinse.

When you shampoo, do not use the scrubbing motion so often used when washing human hair.

Rather, work the soap in the hair by following the lie of the coat. Thorough rinsing is important. Soap residue will make your next grooming session a nightmare. Twigs and leaves will be attracted to the residue and stick in the coat. These little tricks will make your grooming work easier. The same holds true for toweling dry. Do not rub back and forth, instead pat dry and squeeze dry. Again, the typical back and forth motion of toweling of hair will raise havoc with the coat.

Brushing your Wheaten Terrier's coat while blow drying will help the coat stay in place and look fresh longer.

After toweling dry, put the dog on the table and gently comb through the wet coat. If it is a warm summer day, you can take him outside to dry "au naturel." If the weather discourages this, blow the coat dry with a hair dryer on medium heat while you brush, and you will have a beautifully clean and brushed Wheaten. Brushing while you dry will help the coat "hold" and look fresh longer than the "outdoor" method and make your job of trimming easier. Either way, you can't beat a clean Wheaten!

TRIMMING

The best time to trim your Wheaten is when he is clean. Dirt and oil will dull your scissors, and "clumpy" coats won't trim as nicely. While space does not allow me to take you, step by step, through the process of scissoring your Wheaten into an attractive representative of the breed, I urge you to contact the Soft Coated Wheaten Terrier Club of America to procure the Grooming Chart, the Owner's Manual, and addresses for the grooming videos.

At a minimum, the feet, ears, stomach, groin and rear end of your Wheaten need to be relieved of hair on a regular basis. Thinning some of the forelock over the eyes will allow your Wheaten a clearer view through his thatch of hair. All such grooming will improve his well-being.

Remove the hair from between the pads of each foot. You may use your regular scissors or you may

Your Soft Coated Wheaten Terrier's coat must be trimmed on a regular basis for sanitary reasons as well as to improve his overall health and well being.

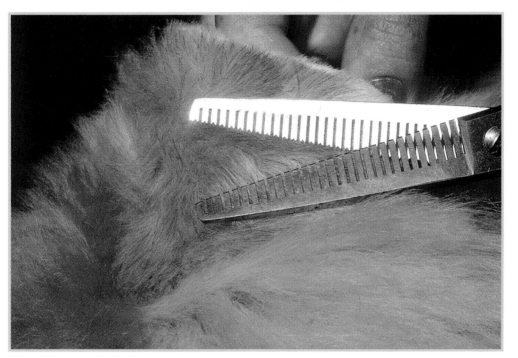

procure a pair of cosmetic nail scissors that are small and have blunted ends. Then, with the dog standing on that leg, trim the long hair draping beyond the circumference of the foot. When completed, the lower leg and foot should resemble a cylinder.

Whether you wish to leave the ears "feathered" or not is a matter of preference. I find that oils and wax from ears tend to get into the feathering and then the coat on the cheeks, leaving the area a bit oily to the touch and a bit smelly. I shorten the hair on the leather (surface) of the ears, then carefully trim close to the actual edge of the ears.

The stomach and groin area is that area between the rear legs and forward to the sternum (the point

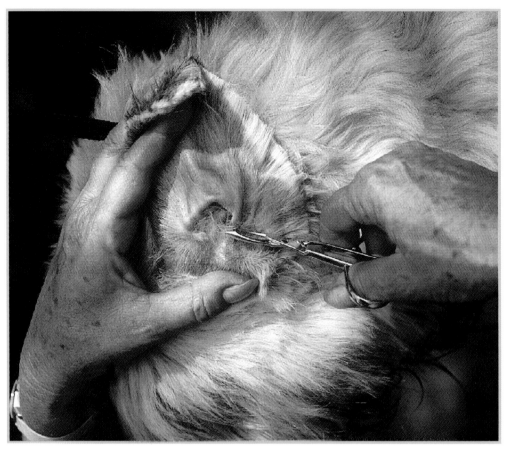

where the ribs actually join). I clip all the hair from that area. This area can easily mat and will often turn a reddish-brown color, both incurred by the dog frequently cleaning that area. Remove all this problematical hair and you will also have a better chance to spot skin problems or a flea infestation, as these little critters seem to like this area of the dog.

For sanitary reasons, the area around the anus should be kept clear of hair. For the same reason, remove any long "flag" on your dog's tail.

Either you or your veterinarian must deal with toenail clipping and removal of hair from the ear canal. Both jobs must be done regularly, especially the nails. Most terriers, and other breeds who were bred to dig for game, come equipped with nails that grow long and fast. If allowed to grow too long, these nails will often split or tear off, causing a great deal of pain and bleeding. Ideally, nails should be trimmed just a bit every seven to ten days to keep them short. If you trim them monthly, you need to trim a lot more off the ends. This is much more difficult to do without cutting the

The hair around your Wheaten's ears must be trimmed regularly and the ear canals kept clean and free of waxy build-up.

quick of the nail and causing the nail to bleed. Pulling out the hair in the ear canal will minimize the amount of oils that tend to permeate the area. In doing this, risk of fungus infections caused by the dark moist conditions will also be minimized. For this job either tweezers or a hemostat will work. Your breeder or your vet can give you lessons in nail trimming and removal of hair from the ear canal.

It is important to realize that dental health should be a factor in your dog's well-being. Many breeders scrape their dogs' teeth monthly. Giving the dog toys specifically geared to canine oral health, such as Nylabone® products will be helpful, but only if the dog is interested in chewing on those toys. There are a variety of these toys from which to choose. Some, like Nylafloss® are designed to massage the gums, some are designed to remove calcified tarter, and some, like the Plaque Attacker® from Nylabone® are designed to remove food particles and plaque. Keep alert to the condition of your dog's teeth and gums, especially as he gets older.

One thing is certain — there is nothing like a clean Wheaten!

TRAINING YOUR SOFT COATED WHEATEN TERRIER

HOUSEBREAKING

I have mentioned crates, and crate training several times. I cannot stress enough how important a crate is, not only for housebreaking, but for your puppy's safety and your peace of mind.

A crate is your dog's bedroom and traveling suite, his safe retreat, if you will. In the wild, the canine

If you take your puppy to the same place to eliminate every time, he'll know what is expected of him. Reinforce what he's learned by praising him when he relieves himself in the correct area.

Your Softie will look to you his owner for the love and guidance he needs to become a well-disciplined and valued family member.

species will find a secluded and covered nest in which he will feel protected enough to sleep in and to raise young. The crate will quickly become your Wheaten's den or lair. A dog will not "mess" in his den. He will be in a safe place while you are away and unable to get into mischief, or worse, get into something that could make him sick.

The key to housebreaking a puppy hinges on two principles: a steady routine and vigilance. Set up a schedule of feeding times, play times, and nap times for your puppy. This will help the youngster to understand what is expected with a minimum of accidents. A young puppy needs to eliminate when he awakens from sleep, when he finishes a meal, and after about 15 to 20 minutes of play. If you follow this routine and watch the puppy and his body language, you may be able to avoid accidents. For the first few weeks, restrict water intake an hour before going out for the last time. All this will make your job easier and speeds up the training process. If you notice the puppy stop his playing to sniff around, get him outside. Use a word or phrase such as "outside" or "let's go outside" when you take him out to do his business. When the puppy does as hoped, praise him lavishly. Keep a

Because of his short attention span, make sure to limit the time spent on your puppy's training sessions. This Wheaten pup pooped out in no time at all!

close eye on the puppy the first week or so. If you catch your puppy in the act, it is much more effective than finding the mistake ten minutes later. It may take a bit of effort to be so very watchful, but if you can avoid accidents or catch them as they are happening, your work will be much more successful and much sooner. Your puppy will very soon learn to look at the door, or walk to the door, then perhaps look expectantly at you. Learn to read your puppy. He is busy reading you all the time.

If you are busy making dinner or answering the phone, put the puppy in his crate or assign the vigil to another member of the family. You may be able to do two things well, but not if one thing is watching a puppy—they are very quick.

Paper training only serves to confuse a puppy and double your work. It is a two-stage process of allowing the puppy to eliminate indoors on the papers, followed by removal of the papers and an abrupt change of rules.

With persistent training, your Wheaten Terrier will soon be letting you know when he needs to go outside. Owner, Cheryl Turner Fogarty.

The crate is where your Wheaten belongs if you leave the house. Should you decide to close him in a small room, such as bathroom or laundry room, you will be delaying the training and possibly be putting your puppy at risk. Any room is large enough for a puppy to make a mess and avoid stepping in it. In essence, you have given him the equivalent of a three-room suite—bedroom, playroom, and bathroom. He could conceivably get into something harmful; he will definitely find something to destroy. Use the crate.

Give him a couple of his toys and put him safely away. He can't get into trouble or into danger when he is put in his private little lair.

The crate is not a cage, nor is it a prison, and should not be used as such. Treat it as a private room. If you have children, the crate is an excellent way to allow the puppy to rest. Teach your children that the puppy should be left alone when he goes into his "room" to take a nap. It should be a safe haven. I feed my dogs in their crates, partly because it avoids quarrels over the food dishes and partly because it enhances their attachment to their private quarters. Each dog has his own space and, if allowed freedom in the house, he will always return to his "house" to take a snooze.

It is important that your Wheaten learn to wear his collar and leash when walking outside. Owners, the Donahue family.

When you travel with your pet, the crate is his home away from home and his personal safety belt. Many a dog has walked out of his crate after a car accident. Most crates are sturdy enough to withstand a strong impact. Dogs in crates are welcome visitors. You don't have to worry about the condition of a motel room when you return from dinner. Your dog will feel more comfortable in strange surroundings if he is in his familiar lair. It allows him security and a feeling of continuity.

By limiting your puppy's freedom, you can prevent accidents from happening. If you cannot supervise your Wheaten, put him in his crate or in a fenced area.

Dogs instinctively want to leave a "mark" when in a new place to let other dogs know they were there. This urge to leave a scent applies to both sexes. Whether you and your dog are staying with relatives, friends, or at a motel, crating your dog will improve your relationship with your hosts. And you won't be surprised by any "damage charges" added on your motel bill.

Should you decide on an older dog, the crate should still be used. The breeder's dog will be used to crates and he will look upon the crate as a familiar friend in unfamiliar territory. Wean the dog out of the

crate gradually, giving him more freedom and allowing him to investigate a new room—under your supervision. The instinct to mark new territory will apply to your house. The less new territory thrown upon a dog, the easier for him to accept changes. Remember, while puppies have no developed sense of routine, an adult dog has lived with a pattern for a year or more and must deal with learning and adopting your lifestyle. Allow him to concentrate on getting to know you and adjusting to your particular routine, and one or two rooms only, in the beginning.

In a few short weeks, your Wheaten should be feeling quite at home. In fact, he may drop his "houseguest manners" and decide that it is time that he tasted that delectable-looking chair that he has been walking by these few weeks. Or perhaps he caught the fading scent of a past dog—maybe he should check that out. Oh boy, little Billie left a present for the new dog—his sneakers are in the hall. The moral of this story is don't be too quick to wean your new dog away from the crate. If you leave the house for a number of hours, crate your dog. Trust him for short trips before you allow him total freedom. A Wheaten is quick to learn anything you wish to teach him. Be patient and allow him to earn his freedom gradually.

This Soft Coated Wheaten Terrier demonstrates the versatility and agility of the breed by flying over the bar jump. Owner, Elizabeth Sorenson.

Opposite: Casey O'Malley obeys the sit/stay command from his owner Carol Shaltz.

A Wheaten will look to you for direction. He depends upon you for companionship. He is quick, adept at reading body language and sensitive to nuances. This makes him a very good candidate for obedience work and more.

If you have never attended obedience classes, I might suggest that you attend one or two classes prior to bringing your Wheaten so you can stay ahead of him. You will be learning just as much as your Wheaten. It will be your job to work with him every day to practice

The versatile Soft Coated Wheaten Terrier excels at any endeavor he tries. This Wheaten owned by Shelly Sumner heads after ducks in a herding test.

what you have learned in the latest class. This will instill the commands and responses and prepare you both for the new commands you will be learning in the next class. This training gives your Wheaten purpose and interest, while creating a strong bond between you, the handler, and your dog. Most Wheatens I have owned enjoyed obedience work. It was undivided attention with a good deal of praise. I am told they enjoy tracking work, and, if I know my breed, I think they would really enjoy agility work. Agility is an obstacle course comprised of jumps, tunnels, lines of poles to weave through, a seesaw to walk up and then down, plus more. All of this is done at high speed, and with a differently arranged course each time.

Therapy work is something Wheatens have been doing for a long time. The breed has been used over the years in nursing homes as well as homes for the mentally and emotionally challenged. Their keen perception makes the breed a natural for this type of work. The breed is born gregarious, and it is a wonderful opportunity for them and very rewarding work for both of you. I sold one of my pups to a lady who was hearing-impaired and she trained the Wheaten to let her know if the phone was ringing or someone was at the door.

It would seem that the term "all-purpose" knows almost no bounds. This breed likes going in the car, being with you, and learning. The breed wants to work, and will go so far as to look for something to do. I have known of Wheaten Terriers who track, hunt, herd, retrieve, compete in obedience trials, do therapy work, go boating, give "bunny alerts," raise kittens as their own, and even water-ski. I have known of Wheatens who have held a burglar at bay, who have protected their owners, and even rescued their owners.

To the many people who own a Soft Coated Wheaten Terrier, the primary attractions of this blond beauty are his grace and his Irish warmth and charm. Owning a Wheaten is a commitment but it is also an adventure; a dedicated companionship and also a constant party. Living with a Wheaten is being infected by his happy nature and his keen insight; it is also continual brushing and combing. The Wheaten Terrier is not quite like any other breed I have known. Perhaps, in the near future, every Soft Coated Wheaten Terrier will have to be sold with a warning label: "Caution: Owning a Wheaten can lead to addiction."

Participating in obedience not only produces a well-mannered Wheaten but also creates a stronger bond between dog and owner.

YOUR HEALTHY
SOFT COATED
WHEATEN TERRIER

Dogs, like all other animals, are capable of contracting problems and diseases that, in most cases, are easily avoided by sound husbandry—meaning well-bred and well-cared-for animals are less prone to developing diseases and problems than are carelessly bred and neglected animals. Your knowledge of how to avoid problems is far more valuable than all of the books and advice on how to cure them. Respectively, the only person you should listen to about treatment is your vet. Veterinarians don't have all the answers, but at least they are trained to analyze and treat illnesses, and are aware of the full implications of treatments. This does not mean a few old remedies aren't good standbys when all else fails, but in most cases modern science provides the best treatments for disease.

Opposite: As a responsible Soft Coated Wheaten Terrier owner, you should have a basic understanding of the medical problems that effect the breed.

PHYSICAL EXAMS

Your puppy should receive regular physical examinations or check-ups. These come in two forms. One is obviously performed by your vet, and the other is a day-to-day procedure that should be done by you. Apart from the fact the exam will highlight any problem at an early stage, it is an excellent way of socializing the pup to being handled.

To do the physical exam yourself, start at the head and work your way around the body. You are looking for any sign of lesions, or any indication of parasites on the pup. The most common parasites are fleas and ticks.

Maintaining healthy teeth and gums is an important part of your dog's general care.

HEALTHY TEETH AND GUMS

Chewing is instinctual. Puppies chew so that their teeth and jaws grow strong and healthy as they develop. As the permanent teeth begin to emerge, it is painful and annoying to the puppy, and puppy owners must recognize that their new charges need something safe upon which to chew. Unfortunately, once the puppy's permanent teeth have emerged and settled solidly into the jaw, the chewing instinct does not fade. Adult dogs instinctively need to clean their teeth, massage their gums, and exercise their jaws through chewing.

It is necessary for your dog to have clean teeth. You should take your dog to the veterinarian at least once a year to have his teeth cleaned and to have his mouth examined for any sign of oral disease. Although dogs do not get cavities in the same way humans do, dogs' teeth accumulate tartar, and more quickly than humans do! Veterinarians recommend brushing your dog's teeth daily. But who can find time to brush their dog's teeth daily? The accumulation of tartar and plaque on our dog's teeth when not removed can cause irritation and eventually erode the enamel and finally destroy the teeth. Advanced cases, while destroying the teeth, bring on gingivitis and periodontitis, two very serious conditions that can affect the dog's internal organs as well...to say nothing about bad breath!

Since everyone can't brush their dog's teeth daily or get to the veterinarian often enough for him to scale

Safe chew toys, like Nylabones®, can promote oral health, as well as keep your Wheaten busy.

the dog's teeth, providing the dog with something safe to chew on will help maintain oral hygeine. Chew devices from Nylabone® keep dogs' teeth clean, but they also provide an excellent resource for entertainment and relief of doggie tensions. Nylabone® products give your dog something to do for an hour or two every day and during that hour or two, your dog will be taking an active part in keeping his teeth and gums healthy…without even realizing it! That's invaluable to your dog, and valuable to you!

Nylabone® provides fun bones, challenging bones, and *safe* bones. It is an owner's responsibility to recognize safe chew toys from dangerous ones. Your dog will chew and devour anything you give him. Dogs must not be permitted to chew on items that they can break. Pieces of broken objects can do internal damage to a dog, besides ripping the dog's mouth. Cheap plastic or rubber toys can cause stoppage in the intestines; such stoppages are operable only if caught immediately.

The most obvious choices, in this case, may be the worst choice. Natural beef bones were not designed for chewing and cannot take too much pressure from the sides. Due to the abrasive nature of these bones, they should be offered most sparingly. Knuckle bones, though once very popular for dogs, can be easily

Yearly dental examinations by your veterinarian are essential to your dog's overall health.

Be sure to check your Wheaten's coat thoroughly for parasites, like ticks and fleas, when he comes in from playing outdoors.

chewed up and eaten by dogs. At the very least, digestion is interrupted; at worst, the dog can choke or suffer from intestinal blockage.

When a dog chews hard on a Nylabone®, little bristle-like projections appear on the surface of the bone. These help to clean the dog's teeth and add to the gum-massaging. Given the chemistry of the nylon, the bristle can pass through the dog's intestinal tract without effect. Since nylon is inert, no microorganism can grow on it, and it can be washed in soap and water or sterilized in boiling water or in an autoclave.

For the sake of your dog, his teeth and your own peace of mind, provide your dog with Nylabones®. They have 100 variations from which to choose.

FIGHTING FLEAS

Fleas are very mobile and may be red, black, or brown in color. The adults suck the blood of the host, while the larvae feed on the feces of the adults, which is rich in blood. Flea "dirt" may be seen on the pup as very tiny clusters of blackish specks that look like freshly ground pepper. The eggs of fleas may be laid on the puppy, though they are more commonly laid off the host in a favorable place, such as the bedding. They normally hatch in 4 to 21 days, depending on the temperature, but they can survive for up to 18 months if temperature conditions are not favorable. The larvae are maggot-like and molt a couple of times before forming pupae, which can survive long periods until the temperature, or the vibration of a nearby host, causes them to emerge and jump on a host.

There are a number of effective treatments available, and you should discuss them with your veterinarian, then follow all instructions for the one you choose. Any treatment will involve a product for your puppy or dog and one for the environment, and will require diligence on your part to treat all areas and thoroughly clean your home and yard until the infestation is eradicated.

THE TROUBLE WITH TICKS

Ticks are arthropods of the spider family, which means they have eight legs (though the larvae have six). They bury their headparts into the host and gorge on its blood. They are easily seen as small grain-like creatures sticking out from the skin. They are often picked up when dogs play in fields, but may also arrive in your yard via wild animals—even birds—or stray cats and dogs. Some ticks are species-specific, others are more adaptable and will host on many species.

The cat flea is the most common flea of dogs. It starts feeding soon after it makes contact with the dog.

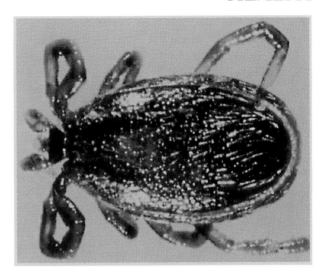

The deer tick is the most common carrier of Lyme disease. Photo courtesy of Virbac Laboratories, Inc., Fort Worth, Texas.

The most troublesome type of tick is the deer tick, which spreads the deadly Lyme disease that can cripple a dog (or a person). Deer ticks are tiny and very hard to detect. Often, by the time they're big enough to notice, they've been feeding on the dog for a few days—long enough to do their damage. Lyme disease was named for the area of the United States in which it was first detected—Lyme, Connecticut— but has now been diagnosed in almost all parts of the U.S. Your veterinarian can advise you of the danger to your dog(s) in your area, and may suggest your dog be vaccinated for Lyme. Always go over your dog with a fine-toothed flea comb when you come in from walking through any area that may harbor deer ticks, and if your dog is acting unusually sluggish or sore, seek veterinary advice.

Attempts to pull a tick free will invariably leave the headpart in the pup, where it will die and cause an infected wound or abscess. The best way to remove ticks is to dab a strong saline solution, iodine, or alcohol on them. This will numb them, causing them to loosen their hold, at which time they can be removed with forceps. The wound can then be cleaned and covered with an antiseptic ointment. If ticks are common in your area, consult with your vet for a suitable pesticide to be used in kennels, on bedding, and on the puppy or dog.

INSECTS AND OTHER OUTDOOR DANGERS

There are many biting insects, such as mosquitoes, that can cause discomfort to a puppy. Many diseases are transmitted by the males of these species.

A pup can easily get a grass seed or thorn lodged between his pads or in the folds of his ears. These may go unnoticed until an abscess forms.

This is where your daily check of the puppy or dog will do a world of good. If your puppy has been playing in long grass or places where there may be thorns, pine needles, wild animals, or parasites, the check-up is a wise precaution.

SKIN DISORDERS

Apart from problems associated with lesions created by biting pests, a puppy may fall foul to a number of other skin disorders. Examples are ringworm, mange, and eczema. Ringworm is not caused by a worm, but is a fungal infection. It manifests itself as a sore-looking bald circle. If your puppy should have any form of bald patches, let your veterinarian check him over; a microscopic examination can confirm the condition. Many old remedies for ringworm exist, such as iodine, carbolic acid, formalin, and other tinctures, but modern drugs are superior.

There are many dangers in the great outdoors that your dog can encounter, so closely supervise him when he is outside.

Fungal infections can be very difficult to treat, and even more difficult to eradicate, because of the spores. These can withstand most treatments, other than burning, which is the best thing to do with bedding once the condition has been confirmed.

Mange is a general term that can be applied to many skin conditions where the hair falls out and a flaky crust develops and falls away.

Often, dogs will scratch themselves, and this invariably is worse than the original condition, for it opens lesions that are then subject to viral, fungal, or parasitic attack. The cause of the problem can be various species of mites. These either live on skin debris and the hair follicles, which they destroy, or they bury themselves just beneath the skin and feed on the tissue. Applying general remedies from pet stores is not recommended because it is essential to identify the type of mange before a specific treatment is effective.

Eczema is another non-specific term applied to many skin disorders. The condition can be brought about in many ways. Sunburn, chemicals, allergies to foods, drugs, pollens, and even stress can all produce a deterioration of the skin and coat. Given the range of causal factors, treatment can be difficult because the problem is one of identification. It is a case of taking each possibility at a time and trying to correctly diagnose the matter. If the cause is of a dietary nature then you must remove one item at a time in order to find out if the dog is allergic to a given food. It could, of course, be the lack of a nutrient that is the problem, so if the condition persists, you should consult your veterinarian.

INTERNAL DISORDERS

It cannot be overstressed that it is very foolish to attempt to diagnose an internal disorder without the advice of a veterinarian. Take a relatively common problem such as diarrhea. It might be caused by nothing more serious than the puppy hogging a lot of food or eating something that it has never previously eaten. Conversely, it could be the first indication of a potentially fatal disease. It's up to your veterinarian to make the correct diagnosis.

The following symptoms, especially if they accompany each other or are progressively added to earlier symptoms, mean you should visit the veterinarian right away:

Continual vomiting. All dogs vomit from time to time and this is not necessarily a sign of illness. They will eat grass to induce vomiting. It is a natural cleansing process common to many carnivores. However, continued vomiting is a clear sign of a problem. It may be a blockage in the pup's intestinal tract, it may be induced by worms, or it could be due to any number of diseases.

Diarrhea. This, too, may be nothing more than a temporary condition due to many factors. Even a change of home can induce diarrhea, because this often stresses the pup, and invariably there is some change in the diet. If it persists more than 48 hours then something is amiss. If blood is seen in the feces, waste no time at all in taking the dog to the vet.

Running eyes and/or nose. A pup might have a chill and this will cause the eyes and nose to weep. Again, this should quickly clear up if the puppy is placed in a warm environment and away from any drafts. If it does not, and especially if a mucous discharge is seen, then the pup has an illness that must be diagnosed.

Coughing. Prolonged coughing is a sign of a problem, usually of a respiratory nature.

Wheezing. If the pup has difficulty breathing and makes a wheezing sound when breathing, then something Is wrong.

Cries when attempting to defecate or urinate. This might only be a minor problem due to the hard state of the feces, but it could be more serious, especially if the pup cries when urinating.

Cries when touched. Obviously, if you do not handle a puppy with care he might yelp. However, if he cries even when lifted gently, then he has an internal problem that becomes apparent when pressure is applied to a given area of the body. Clearly, this must be diagnosed.

Refuses food. Generally, puppies and dogs are greedy creatures when it comes to feeding time. Some might be more fussy, but none should refuse more than one meal. If they go for a number of hours without showing any interest in their food, then something is not as it should be.

General listlessness. All puppies have their off days when they do not seem their usual cheeky, mischievous selves. If this condition persists for more than two days then there is little doubt of a problem. They may not show any of the signs listed, other than perhaps a reduced interest in their food. There are many diseases that can develop internally without displaying obvious clinical signs. Blood, fecal, and other tests are needed in order to identify the disorder before it reaches an advanced state that may not be treatable.

WORMS

There are many species of worms, and a number of these live in the tissues of dogs and most other animals. Many create no problem at all, so you are not even aware they exist. Others can be tolerated in small levels, but become a major problem if they number more than a few. The most common types seen in dogs are roundworms and tapeworms. While roundworms are the greater problem, tapeworms require an intermediate host so are more easily eradicated.

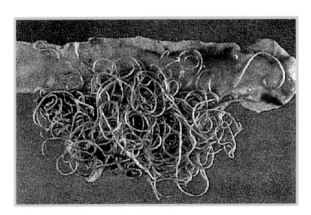

Roundworms are spaghetti-like worms that cause a pot-bellied appearance and dull coat, along with more severe symptoms, such as diarrhea and vomiting. Photo courtesy of Merck AgVet.

Roundworms of the species *Toxocara canis* infest the dog. They may grow to a length of 8 inches (20 cm) and look like strings of spaghetti. The worms feed on the digesting food in the pup's intestines. In chronic cases the puppy will become pot-bellied, have diarrhea, and will vomit. Eventually, he will stop eating, having passed through the stage when he always seems hungry. The worms lay eggs in the puppy and these pass out in his feces. They are then either ingested by the pup, or they are eaten by mice, rats, or beetles. These may then be eaten by the puppy and the life cycle is complete.

Larval worms can migrate to the womb of a pregnant bitch, or to her mammary glands, and this is how they pass to the puppy. The pregnant bitch can be wormed, which will help. The pups can, and should,

Whipworms are hard to find unless you strain your dog's feces, and this is best left to a veterinarian. Pictured here are adult whipworms.

be wormed when they are about two weeks old. Repeat worming every 10 to 14 days and the parasites should be removed. Worms can be extremely dangerous to young puppies, so you should be sure the pup is wormed as a matter of routine.

Tapeworms can be seen as tiny rice-like eggs sticking to the puppy's or dog's anus. They are less destructive, but still undesirable. The eggs are eaten by mice, fleas, rabbits, and other animals that serve as intermediate hosts. They develop into a larval stage and the host must be eaten by the dog in order to complete the chain. Your vet will supply a suitable remedy if tapeworms are seen or suspected. There are other worms, such as hookworms and whipworms, that are also blood suckers. They will make a pup anemic, and blood might be seen in the feces, which can be examined by the vet to confirm their presence. Cleanliness in all matters is the best preventative measure for all worms.

Heartworm infestation in dogs is passed by mosquitoes but can be prevented by a monthly (or daily) treatment that is given orally. Talk to your vet about the risk of heartworm in your area.

BLOAT (GASTRIC DILATATION)

This condition has proved fatal in many dogs, especially large and deep-chested breeds, such as the Weimaraner and the Great Dane. However, any dog can get bloat. It is caused by swallowing air during exercise, food/water gulping or another strenuous task. As many believe, it is not the result of flatulence. The stomach of an affected dog twists, disallowing food and blood flow and resulting in harmful toxins being released into the bloodstream. Death can easily follow if the condition goes undetected.

The best preventative measure is not to feed large meals or exercise your puppy or dog immediately after he has eaten. Veterinarians recommend feeding three smaller meals per day in an elevated feeding rack, adding water to dry food to prevent gulping, and not offering water during mealtimes.

VACCINATIONS

Every puppy, purebred or mixed breed, should be vaccinated against the major canine diseases. These are distemper, leptospirosis, hepatitis, and canine parvovirus. Your puppy may have received a temporary vaccination against distemper before you purchased him, but be sure to ask the breeder to be sure.

The age at which vaccinations are given can vary, but will usually be when the pup is 8 to 12 weeks old. By this time any protection given to the pup by antibodies received from his mother via her initial milk feeds will be losing their strength.

The puppy's immune system works on the basis that the white blood cells engulf and render harmless

Rely on your veterinarian for the most effectual vaccination schedule for your Soft Coated Wheaten Terrier puppy.

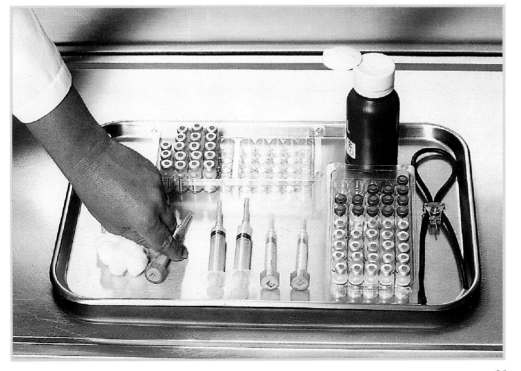

attacking bacteria. However, they must first recognize a potential enemy.

Vaccines are either dead bacteria or they are live, but in very small doses. Either type prompts the pup's defense system to attack them. When a large attack then comes (if it does), the immune system recognizes it and massive numbers of lymphocytes (white blood corpuscles) are mobilized to counter the attack. However, the ability of the cells to recognize these dangerous viruses can diminish over a period of time. It is therefore useful to provide annual reminders about the nature of the enemy. This is done by means of booster injections that keep the immune system on its alert. Immunization is not 100-percent guaranteed to be successful, but is very close. Certainly it is better than giving the puppy no protection.

Dogs are subject to other viral attacks, and if these are of a high-risk factor in your area, then your vet will suggest you have the puppy vaccinated against these as well.

Your puppy or dog should also be vaccinated against the deadly rabies virus. In fact, in many places it is illegal for your dog not to be vaccinated. This is to protect your dog, your family, and the rest of the animal population from this deadly virus that infects the nervous system and causes dementia and death.

ACCIDENTS
All puppies will get their share of bumps and bruises due to the rather energetic way they play. These will usually heal themselves over a few days. Small cuts should be bathed with a suitable disinfectant and then smeared with an antiseptic ointment. If a cut looks more serious, then stem the flow of blood with a towel or makeshift tourniquet and rush the pup to the veterinarian. Never apply so much pressure to the wound that it might restrict the flow of blood to the limb.

In the case of burns you should apply cold water or an ice pack to the surface. If the burn was due to a chemical, then this must be washed away with copious amounts of water. Apply petroleum jelly, or any vegetable oil, to the burn. Trim away the hair if need be. Wrap the dog in a blanket and rush him to the vet. The pup may go into shock, depending on the severity of the burn, and this will result in a lowered blood pressure, which is dangerous and the reason the pup must receive immediate veterinary attention.

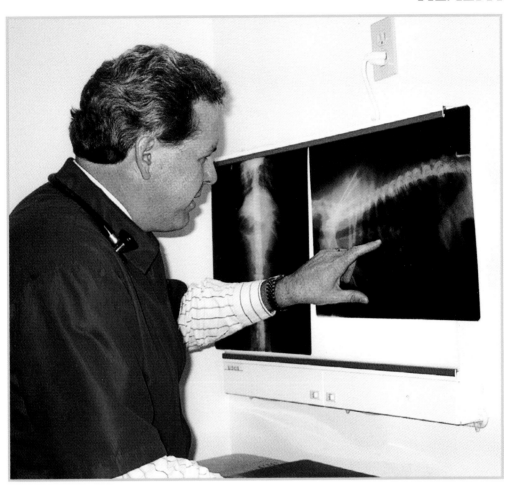

It is a good idea to x-ray the chest and abdomen on any dog hit by a car.

If a broken limb is suspected then try to keep the animal as still as possible. Wrap your pup or dog in a blanket to restrict movement and get him to the veterinarian as soon as possible. Do not move the dog's head so it is tilting backward, as this might result in blood entering the lungs.

Do not let your pup jump up and down from heights, as this can cause considerable shock to the joints. Like all youngsters, puppies do not know when enough is enough, so you must do all their thinking for them.

Provided you apply strict hygiene to all aspects of raising your puppy, and you make daily checks on his physical state, you have done as much as you can to safeguard him during his most vulnerable period. Routine visits to your veterinarian are also recommended, especially while the puppy is under one year of age. The vet may notice something that did not seem important to you.

PET OWNERS & BLOOD PRESSURE

Over the past few years, several scientific studies have documented many health benefits of having pets in our lives. At the State University of New York at Buffalo, for example, Dr. Karen Allen and her colleagues have focused on how physical reactions to psychological stress are influenced by the presence of pets. One such study compared the effect of pets with that of a person's close friend and reported pets to be dramatically better than friends at providing unconditional support. Blood pressure was monitored throughout the study, and, on average, the blood pressure of people under stress who were *with* their pets was 112/75, as compared to 140/95 when they were with the self-selected friends. Heart rate differences were also significantly lower when participants were with their pets. A follow-up study included married couples and looked at the stress-reducing effect of pets versus *spouses*, and found, once again, that pets were dramatically more successful than other people in reducing cardiovascular reactions to stress. An interesting discovery made in this study was that when the spouse and pet were *both* present, heart rate and blood pressure came down dramatically.

Other work by the same researchers has looked at the role of pets in moderating age-related increases in blood pressure. In a study that followed 100 women (half in their 20s and half in their 70s) over six months, it was found that elderly women with few social contacts and *no* pets had blood pressures that were significantly higher (averages of 145/95 compared to 120/80) than elderly women with their beloved pets but few *human* contacts. In other words, elderly women with pets, but no friends, had blood pressures that closely reflected the blood pressures of young women.

This series of studies demonstrates that pets can play an important role in how we handle everyday stress, and shows that biological aging cannot be fully understood without a consideration of the social factors in our lives.

More than best friends or even spouses, pets have a natural calming effect on their humans.

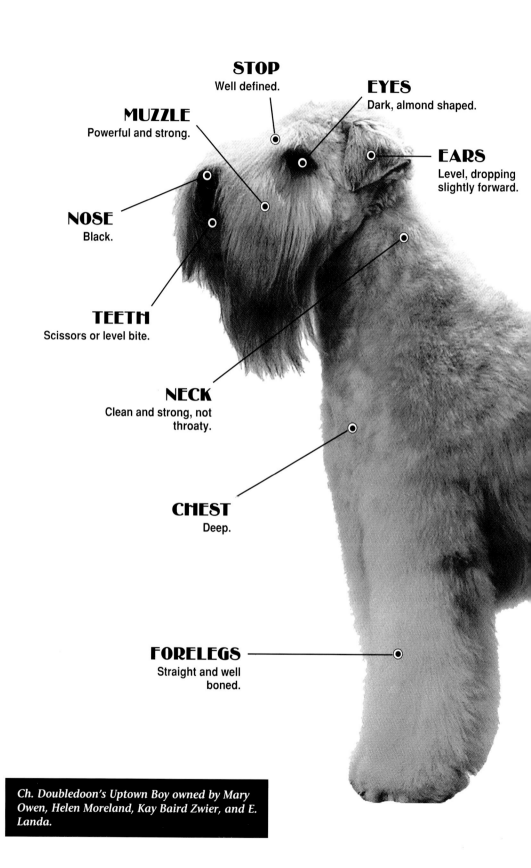

STOP
Well defined.

EYES
Dark, almond shaped.

MUZZLE
Powerful and strong.

EARS
Level, dropping slightly forward.

NOSE
Black.

TEETH
Scissors or level bite.

NECK
Clean and strong, not throaty.

CHEST
Deep.

FORELEGS
Straight and well boned.

Ch. Doubledoon's Uptown Boy owned by Mary Owen, Helen Moreland, Kay Baird Zwier, and E. Landa.